A Bible Study Focused on Fasting

N.A. Rogers

ONESTONE
BIBLICAL RESOURCES

2023 One Stone Press.
All rights reserved. No part of this book may be reproduced in any form without written permission of the publisher.

Published by:
One Stone Press
979 Lovers Lane
Bowling Green, KY 42103

Printed in the United States of America

ISBN (13 Digit): 978-1-941422-82-3

1 (800) 428-0121
www.onestone.com

Contents

Biblical examples of fasting 7
    Christians Fasting 7
    Moses, Elijah and Jesus 7
    Israel Calls for Help 9
    Nazirite Vow 10
    Hannah and Jonathan Refuse to Eat 10
    Saul Requires a Fast 11
    Honor 12
    Mourning and Repentance 13
    David Fasts for Others and Himself 14
    Jezebel Calls for a Fast 14
    King Darius Fasts 15
    Daniel 15
    Ezra Prays and Fasts for Protection 17
    Esther Pleas for the Jews 17
    Ezra and Nehemiah Pray and Fast for Forgiveness. 18
    Anna Looks for the Redemption of Jerusalem 19
    Preparing for Challenges 19
    Saul (Paul) Prays and Fasts 20
    Summary 20

Fasting Expectations 21
    Jews Fast on Day of Atonement 21
    Calls to Repent, Fast 22
    Unacceptable Fasts 22
    God's Expectations 24
    When Jesus Is Not with You. 24
    Fast to the Father 25
    What Is Not Taught to Christians about Fasting: 25

Miscellaneous Points on Fasting 26
    Health Benefits of Fasting. 26
    Fasting in Different Areas and Purposes 27
    Different Source Material 28
    Forced Abstinence 28
    Hermeneutics 28
    How Can Fasting Help? 29
Summary and Concluding Thoughts 30
Appendix 31
    Commonalities of Moses, Elijah, and Jesus 31
    Group Fasts 33
    Individual Fasts 36

Introduction

During a study of the Sermon on the Mount in Matthew, I noticed that fasting was not discussed with the same background and interest as the other topics from Jesus's teachings. It seemed a study that looked at Bible scriptures on fasting might be beneficial.

This discussion begins with who fasted in the Bible, why they fasted, how they fasted, and what was the outcome. After spending time with Bible examples, we discuss Biblical teachings on fasting: what God expected, what made fasts unacceptable, what the Bible does not specify, and some historical and additional general information on fasting.

There are several types of fasts mentioned in the Bible. In some religions, millions of people fast each year. Sometimes ignorance breeds fear. If we learn what the Bible says about fasting, it should help us understand when we could benefit from spiritual fasting. Understanding what is expected of Christians provides a tool to improve our relationship with our Lord.

The reader is strongly encouraged to read the scriptures and put the passage in context. Quotes are from the American Standard version unless noted otherwise.

The objective is to aid understanding and spiritual growth that the use of appropriate fasting can provide. Ultimately, may this study provide an additional tool to improve your relationship with Jehovah.

About the Author

Dr. Rogers grew up in Texas with the benefit of a Christian family and has been a member of the church since her teens. She and her husband are members of Castleberry Church of Christ in Fort Worth, Texas, and are blessed with friends who enjoy studying the Bible. They have three children and five grandchildren. After the youngest child moved out, Dr. Rogers completed a Ph.D. in Finance from the University of North Texas. Currently, she is a professor at a state university.

Dr. Rogers hopes to have a bible study on eunuchs available soon.

Acknowledgement

One of the joys of Bible study is seeing it from new perspectives. This study reflects my understanding of fasting from the scriptures, but it is not the same as I thought 30 years ago. Therefore, if I make mistakes, they are not intentional, and all errors are my own.

There have been several who have encouraged my Bible study that I would like to acknowledge. Rick, Bettie, Brenda, Cassie, Connie, Donna, Genny, Julie, Karen, Kim, Linda, Lorraine, Mary, Michelle, Pat, Natalie, Sandy, Shana, Torri, Vicky and April have been a blessing.

Biblical Examples of Fasting

The Bible mentions fasting in about sixty Bible passages—approximately forty-five times in the Old Testament and twelve to seventeen passages in the New Testament.[1] Groups and individuals fasted for multiple reasons. There are passages describing unacceptable fasts and calls to fast. Several Psalms include fasting. Jews fasted, as did the Ninevites, Medes/Persians, and Christians.

What is your first thought when the Bible mentions spiritual fasting? You may think I can't fast! You may remember Jesus's forty days of fasting in the wilderness or the fasting teaching from the Sermon on the Mount. If you haven't studied fasting very much, it may seem unimportant. It may be healthy for some people, but it takes self-control. Jesus mentions it several times. Let's look at some of the Bible examples of fasting.

Christians Fasting

Two passages have examples of Christians fasting. Several Christians at Antioch were worshiping[2] and fasting (Acts 13:2). During this time, the Holy Spirit asked that Barnabas and (Saul) Paul be sent out among the Gentiles. The church fasted and prayed before laying their hands on Barnabas and Paul and sending them on a journey to share the gospel (Acts 13:3). In Antioch in Pisidia, Iconium, and Derbe, the apostle Paul and Barnabas were successful in developing believers from Jews and Gentiles (Acts 13:48, 14:1, 14:21-23). After significant struggles, they returned to the congregations at Lystra, Iconium, and Antioch Pisidia, where they appointed elders with fasting and prayer.

Moses, Elijah and Jesus

Fasting is first mentioned in the scriptures as an action by Moses when receiving the Ten Commandments from Jehovah (Exodus 34:27-28, Deuteronomy 9:9). When Moses came down from the mountain, he did not find Israel patiently waiting. (Israel was worshipping a golden calf). Moses again fasted forty days and nights and begged Jehovah not to destroy the people and Aaron (Deuteronomy 9:17-20, 10:10-11). God listened to Moses and did not destroy the people. In Deuteronomy 9:25, when Moses is recapping the events, he mentions another time he prayed to Jehovah for forty days

---

1 The range in the New Testament is linked to differences in the King James Versions and other versions.

2 The word used in this passage for worship may also be interpreted ministering.

and nights after Israel rebelled at Kadesh Barnea. The spies had returned, and the people listened to those weak in faith. Israel wanted to return to Egypt rather than go to Canaan. At this rebellion, Moses fasted and prayed for the people, and God listened again.[3]

Moses was raised an Egyptian (forty years) and lived half his life as a shepherd with Jethro (forty years), a priest of Midian (Exodus 2 & 3). Fasting might have been part of religious practices before this mention by Moses, but I could not find any evidence of fasting by the Egyptians or Midianites. Moses was in the presence of Jehovah and seems to take Jesus's comment that "man does not live by food alone..." literally (Matthew 4:4).

The second person mentioned who fasted for forty days and nights was Elijah. After Mount Carmel, where Elijah slew the prophets of Baal (1 Kings 18:20-40), Jezebel swore to kill Elijah. Elijah ran for his life and eventually rested.[4] He was fed by a messenger of God two times, then on the "strength of that food forty days and forty nights," he walked to Mount Horeb (Mount Sinai) (1 Kings 19:1-8): this time the fast prepared Elijah to talk to God. When reading 1 Kings 19:11-19, Elijah felt the wind that broke rocks, an earthquake that shook the mountain, fire, and a voice. God reminded Elijah of his power, listened to Elijah's concerns, and gave him three tasks, including training a successor, Elisha (1 Kings 19:9-18).

Jesus is the third person mentioned to fast forty days and nights.[5] Both Matthew and Luke explain how the Spirit led Jesus into the wilderness, where he ate nothing and dealt with temptations from Satan (Matthew 4:1-11, Luke 4:1-13). Jesus put a low value on food relative to the time spent in spiritual conversation. Sometimes, when fasting comes up in a discussion, we focus on what we miss: food and possibly time eating with others. Jesus tells Satan that the value of time spent with God has greater value than what our physical bodies need. We need spiritual food!

---

3   It is not clear if Moses fasted forty days and nights two, three or possibly four times.
4   While it is not about fasting, 1 Kings 18:46 mentions how the "hand of the Lord was on Elijah," and he ran ahead of Ahab. Now Ahab was on a chariot which was outrunning the rain that was coming, so he wasn't strolling. The vision of Elijah running faster than a chariot makes me appreciate God's sense of humor.
5   In the 1880s, there were professional fasters and several people who reportedly fasted for forty days. Fasting was touted as a cure for many of the diseases. Kerndt, P. R., Naughton, J. L., Driscoll, C. E., & Loxterkamp, D. A. (1982). "Fasting: the History, Pathophysiology and Complications." *Western Journal of Medicine*, 1982. p. 137(5), 379.

After their fasts, it seems Moses, Elijah, and Jesus' understanding aligned with God's. We may have our agenda when we begin a prayer or fast. Hopefully, however, by the end, our thoughts are united with God's. Elijah didn't prepare or plan the fast. It was thrust upon him. It seems God forced Elijah to depend on Him, and Elijah implemented God's plan. Moses gave God's law and implemented the forty years of penance. Jesus fulfilled God's plan after spending forty days fasting and spending time with God. Fasting was part of these leaders' relationship with God. (See Appendix for other commonalities with Moses, Elijah, and Jesus.)

Israel Calls for Help!

There are several examples of Israel seeking God with prayer and fasting when they needed His help. At the end of the book of Judges, the men of Gibeah from the tribe of Benjamin raped and killed a concubine. Men from other tribes in Israel came together to "purge evil from Israel" (Judges 20:13). The army from Israel lost the battle to the Benjamites for two days. Then the army of Israel wept, fasted until evening, offered burnt and peace offerings, and asked the Lord what to do next (Judges 20:26-28). The Lord told them they would win the next day. They set an ambush and eventually won the battle with the Lord's help.

Israel fought with the Philistines for many years. The Philistines frequently won. Israel finally realized that worshiping Baals and Ashtaroths was disobedient, and they needed to return to Jehovah (1 Samuel 7:3). So, Israel gathered at Mizpah, fasted, and confessed their sin against the Lord. The Philistines attacked, the Lord saved Israel, and Samuel set up a stone called Ebenezer (see the song "O Thou Fount of Every Blessing" that refers to Samuel raising Ebenezer to remind the people to turn to Jehovah).

When the Moabites, Ammonites, and Meunites were amassing against Judah, King Jehoshaphat was afraid. He chose to seek Jehovah and proclaimed a fast throughout Judah (2 Chronicles 20:3). Again, God won the battle and the people's praise.

These were dire circumstances, and the people added fasting to their supplications for God's help. There are times when God answered prayers without fasting. So, fasting is not the difference between receiving God's help or not. Isaiah 58:3-6 indicates Israel expects that fasting will make sure that God hears their prayers. Fasting is a way of adding an exclamation point to a prayer to Jehovah.

Nazirite Vow

The Lord allowed men or women to vow to separate their selves to the Lord for a period of time (Numbers 6:1-21). The Nazirite would abstain from grapes, vinegar, wine, and strong drink. The Nazirite would not cut their hair or go near a dead body. When the time was completed, they would take offerings to the temple to end their separation. Many believe that Samson (Judges 13:5), Samuel (1 Samuel 1:11), and John the Baptist (Luke 1:13-15) are examples of Nazirites. Abstinence from any grape product or special diet may be considered a partial fast. Therefore, taking a Nazirite vow would include some self-control. A Nazirite vow is not necessarily a life-long commitment. Vows were for specific events and periods. In Acts 18:18, Paul cuts his hair due to the vow he took and joins with others in observing the Jewish purification process (Acts 21:17-26).

While fasts may eliminate all food and drink, abstinence eliminates some foods or other actions. It is a limited or partial fast. Luke mentions Anna as fasting and praying for most of her life (Luke 2:36-37). Since this cannot be a fast with no food or water, it was probably a partial fast. Daniel abstains from some foods and actions for three weeks (Daniel 10:1-3). For the Nazirite, the actions and drink restrictions help to separate themselves from the routine. Abstaining from a common action or food is as a reminder to focus on the Lord. The required activities are linked to a recognition that God is in charge. Matthew describes John's diet as locusts and wild honey (Matthew 3:4). This would indicate a very limited diet beyond the usual Nazirite vow.

Hannah and Jonathan Refuse to Eat

Psalms 102 begins with the prayer of one afflicted and faint, someone so upset he is not eating and appeals to Jehovah for his pity and favor (grace). Fasting may be natural when we are upset.

Hannah was one of Elkanah's wives, and unlike Peninnah, she did not have any children (1 Samuel 1:1-7). When the family went to make sacrifices at the tabernacle, Peninnah would taunt Hannah. Hannah reacted as many would, she cried and didn't eat. She went to the tabernacle and prayed to God (1 Samuel 1:8-18). Hannah left the tabernacle in peace. She broke her fast and left her anguish with God. She was no longer sad. Hannah is an example of how giving our problems and accepting God's decision gives peace without an immediate answer. Hannah did not leave knowing she would have a child; she left her problems with God. And that was enough to give her peace. In time, Hannah was the mother to four sons and two daughters; the eldest son was Samuel (1 Samuel 2:21).

While fasting may take a conscious effort, there are times when fasting is natural. Deep emotions may create a focus away from physical needs. In Psalm 102:2-4, the psalmist asks for God's attention while they are so distressed they had forgotten to eat. The writer of Psalm 107 shares how sinners realized they are fools, suffered affliction, and their soul loathed food. They cry out to Jehovah and he saves them (Psalms 107:17-19). These Psalms share how fasting and emotional distress are opportune times to reach out to God. This is a time when Hannah shuns food for prayer and took her concern to Jehovah. The result is a soul-bearing prayer and a vow to God. God listened to Hannah and blessed her with children. Hannah fulfilled her vow of giving her son to serve the Lord and not cutting his hair.[6]

Saul was jealous of David and wanted Jonathan to realize he would never be king if David were alive (1 Samuel 20:31). However, Jonathan was David's friend despite Saul's plans. When Jonathan realized that David was not safe around Saul, he was angry and he did not eat (1 Samuel 20:33-34). Jonathan met with David and told him to leave because of Saul's anger. This is another example of someone who fasted from an emotional concern. Jonathan was willing to give his place to the Lord's anointed rather than seek the kingdom for himself.

Saul Requires a Fast

Several times, leaders called for the group or country to fast. Saul called for a fast for his army until he was avenged on his enemies (1 Samuel 14:24-30). Saul didn't call the fast to ask God what to do or to praise God. The fast was called out of anger by Saul. He declares death to any that eat. This fast is not to entreat God's help or learn what God wants. Jonathan didn't hear about the fast, tasted some honey, and Saul almost killed him. Saul used fasting to control others rather than to draw them to God.

Compare Saul's call to Jehoshaphat's call for Judah to fast (2 Chronicles 20). Saul's focus was what he wanted. Jehoshaphat recognized his dependence on Jehovah and the need for His help. He asks for God's judgment on the attacking army (verse 12). God's Spirit came into the group and said, "the battle is not yours, but God's" (verse 15). What an amazing response to Jehoshaphat's plea. When we align our battle with God's, it becomes His battle, and He always wins.

At the end of his reign, God does not answer Saul either by dreams, through the priests with the Urim, or by prophets (1 Samuel 28:6). Saul is scared. He eventually seeks a witch (1 Samuel 28:7). After Samuel tells him what will

---

6   See Nazarite discussion.

happen and why, Saul collapses. Verse 20 of that passage says that Saul had not eaten all day and all night. The verse doesn't say Saul fasted, but he seemed to be trying everything to get a response from Jehovah. God listens, but He will not be manipulated by us for our plans. Saul didn't use prayer and fasting to focus on God, learn God's will, or build a relationship. He tried to use the tools God provided for his own purposes.

Honor

While Jonathan was David's friend, he was loyal to Saul, his father. Saul, Jonathan, and other sons died during a battle with the Philistines. The Philistines gloated and displayed Saul and his son's bodies on the wall of Beth-shan (1 Samuel 31:10).

One of the first actions of the new King Saul had been to come to the aid of the men of Jabesh-Gilead who were being besieged by the Ammonites (1 Samuel 11:1-11). Therefore, when the people of Jabesh-Gilead heard about how the Philistines had abused Saul's body, they traveled all night, brought the bodies home, and burned them. They then buried the bones and fasted for seven days (1 Samuel 31:13 and 1 Chronicles 10:12). These were actions to honor their King and those who had saved them from the Ammonites.

When David heard the news of Saul and Jonathan's deaths he and his men also mourned and fasted until evening (2 Samuel 1:12). David also fasted until evening when Joab (his commander) killed Abner (Saul's former commander) (2 Samuel 3:35). When David was Saul's leader, he and Abner had worked together (1 Samuel 20:25). David and Abner had negotiated an alliance between Israel and Judah after Saul's death. However, Abner had killed one of Joab's brothers during the time Judah and Israel were fighting (2 Samuel 3:30). Therefore, after Abner came to David to finalize the deal uniting Israel with Judah, Joab secretly killed Abner. David fasted until evening to mourn and honor the fallen soldiers (Saul, Jonathan, Abner).

We may have a moment of silence or a memorial to honor someone who has died. It makes us stop from our routine and think about the person and why their loss hurts. Instead of eating a snack or a meal, David, his men, and those from Jabesh-Gilead remembered the deeds of the honored by not eating. There is a verse that says the dead will rest, but their deeds will follow them (Revelation 14:13). David and those from Jabesh-Gilead are an example of how deeds are remembered.

Mourning and Repentance

David's first son with Bathsheba died.[7] The child's death was part of David's punishment for having Uriah killed and David taking Bathsheba as a wife (2 Samuel 12:9-14). Although David knew what Nathan the prophet had said, when the child became sick, David prayed to Jehovah for the child, wept, and fasted for seven days. The answer to David's supplication was "No." Prayer and fasting did not change the outcome.

King Ahab is known for evil, and Elijah proclaims God's judgment to him in 1 Kings 21:21-26. Ahab's reaction is unexpected; he humbled himself before Jehovah. He publicly tore his clothes and fasted, showing his penitence. Our merciful God relented from sending judgment until Ahab died (1 Kings 21:27-29).

Non-Jews also included fasting in their attitude toward Jehovah. Jonah was sent to the Ninevites to tell them of their destruction if they did not repent. To Jonah's surprise, the Ninevites listened, believed God, proclaimed a fast, and repented (Jonah 3:5, 4:1). The king declared a fast, called on God, and told the people to turn from evil and violence. Our God took pity on them, and Jonah became angry (Jonah 4).

There are theories that Jonah's anger was because his prophecy of Nineveh's destruction would not come true, and he would be considered a false prophet. Another theory is that Jonah was angry with how little the Ninevites did for God to relent. While the reasons behind Jonah's anger are not clear, Jonah had also been a recipient of God's mercy. Jonah 2 shares part of his prayer while he was in the fish. While no Bible verse says he fasted while he prayed, the conditions would have been opportune! Jonah was thankful for God's mercy to him but wanted judgment on the Ninevites.

David, King Ahab, the Ninevites, and Jonah, while in the fish, were penitent and humbled themselves. Yet, God's response was not always to grant their prayers. John 3:16 says that God "agapao" the world. Agapao means love, but not an emotional love as much as acting in others' best interest.[8] God heard their prayers and saw their humility. For Ahab and the Assyrians, re-

---

7   David had four sons with Bathsheba, Shimea, Shobab, Nathan and Solomon (1 Chronicles 3:5).
8   According to Strong's Hebrew and Greek Dictionaries, agapao embraces the judgment and deliberate asset of the will as a matter of principle, duty, and propriety. Agapao (agape) is based from the head, while phileo is more from the heart. Similar definition given by W.E. Vine in An Expository Dictionary of New Testament Words with their Precise Meanings for English Readers.

pentance and humility gave them time to change. God answered yes. God does not want anyone to perish (2 Peter 3:9). For David, God continued the punishment he had told David would happen, and David became a better leader.

David Fasts for Others and Himself

In Psalm 35, David afflicted himself with fasting and prayed for friends who were sick. . Then, they gathered against him when he had problems (verses 12-16). He had similar complaints in Psalms 69:10-11. David prayed and fasted for others in difficulties, but his actions were not always reciprocated. In Psalm 109, David decries the wicked and describes himself as poor, needy, and weak through fasting with a stricken heart.

We want justice when others wrong us. We also want recognition when we do something good for others. When we pray and fast for others, and they do us wrong, it is like salt rubbed in a wound. David expresses his frustration but always returns to God's judgments and justice. Jehovah is the one in control, and David realizes that while others should be fair, God does see and respond. Like many of David's psalms, Psalm 109 begins with his wishes but ends with God's.

Jezebel Calls for a Fast

Elijah had given Ahab Jehovah's judgment while he was at Naboth's vineyard (1 Kings 21:18) after the murder of Naboth. Ahab took possession of Naboth's vineyard due to the machinations of Jezebel. She used the pretense of a fast to honor Naboth and gather a crowd. She then had false witnesses charge Naboth with cursing Jehovah and King Ahab. The crowd stoned Naboth, and King Ahab seized his vineyard. (1 Kings 21:1-16).

This story indicates that leaders might call a fast to honor someone. In the book of Esther, Haman suggested that putting on a royal robe and letting an honoree ride a horse through the square while proclaiming this man is honored by the king would be appreciated (Esther 6:1-13). Today, we might have a parade, a banquet honoring someone, or call a building or street by their name. It would be less expensive and easier to have everyone over and not need any food! Maybe Jezebel was cheap as well as evil, but the plan was to have an event, in this case, a fast, to bring a group together. Once the crowd assembled, the 'plants' in the audience would lie about Naboth and stir up the mob to kill him. What a devious plan!

King Darius Fasts

Leaders such as Nebuchadnezzar and King Darius recognized Daniel was a special person (Daniel 1:20, 6:3). Unfortunately, jealous associates wanted Daniel killed and tricked King Darius into signing a law that would cause Daniel to be put to death in a den of lions (Daniel 6:5). King Darius was not pleased with Daniel's exposure to the lion's den due to his injunction (Daniel 6:14). Therefore, King Darius tried to rescue Daniel from the legal mess. When the king put Daniel in the lion's den, he asked God to deliver him. The king stayed up all night fasting and shunned any diversions (abstinence). At dawn, the king hurried to the den and was pleased that Daniel's God had protected him (Daniel 6:18-19). King Darius sent out a decree that the people should tremble and fear before the God of Daniel, for he is the living God, enduring forever; his kingdom shall never be destroyed, and his dominion shall be to the end (Daniel 6:26).

Several cultures beyond that of the Jews fasted. From about 560 to 520 B.C., Greek philosophers such as Pythagoras, Abaris, and Epimenides wrote about fasting and the virtues received by self-discipline.[9] Confucius, born around 550 B.C., also taught abstinence (fasting) in China. So, while the Hebrews were in Babylon, the Greek and the Asian cultures were expanding. Fasting was discussed and practiced by their philosophical leaders. It is unknown how much other cultures influenced Biblical areas or if the fasting practiced by Biblical characters influenced other cultures. However, fasting for self-discipline went well beyond the Jewish culture.

Daniel

Daniel read from the prophet Jeremiah that it would be 70 years before Israel would return to Jerusalem. He then fasted and prayed for Jerusalem (Daniel 9:2-19). This was during the time when Darius, the son of Ahasuerus, was king of the Chaldeans. Gabriel, a messenger from God, responds to Daniel in the evening to help him understand Jerusalem's fate (Daniel 9:20-27).

Later in Daniel 10, during the reign of Cyrus, Daniel mourns and has a limited fast where he eats no delicacies, meat, or wine and does not anoint with oil for three weeks (Daniel 10:3). While beside the river, he sees a vision and a messenger from God comes to him. The messenger says that he came be

---

[9] Kerndt, P. R., Naughton, J. L., Driscoll, C. E., & Loxterkamp, D. A. (1982). Fasting: the History, Pathophysiology and Complications. *Western Journal of Medicine*, 137(5), 379

cause Daniel had 'afflicted' himself and set his heart to understand (Daniel 10:12). These are the rare events when fasting and praying resulted in a visit from a messenger from God.

The 'Daniel Fast' has a following with several books, recipes, and suggestions on duplicating Daniel's diet and prayer for 21 days. The spiritual and health benefit is mentioned by those participating. A modern 'Daniel fast' allows fruits, vegetables, whole grains, legumes, nuts, seeds and oil. It has been reported to provide health benefits similar to a vegan diet. A study of participants found that those participating in the Daniel fast lowered several cardiac, metabolic factors, and cholesterol by approximately 19%. While the abstinence Daniel practiced may have physical benefits, the spiritual benefit includes the humility and heart of Daniel.

Daniel was part of the royal children brought to Babylon by King Nebuchadnezzar (Daniel 1:3). He and his friends, Shadrach, Meshack, and Abednego, asked to abstain from the King's wine and "dainties." Therefore, Daniel and his friends refrained from the King's food, drank water, and ate vegetables. So, Daniel learned self-discipline and abstinence early.

Note: The books of the Bible are not all in chronological order. Paul's letters in the New Testament are arranged based on length, not when he wrote them. Since scrolls did not have "copy and paste" options, even events within a book may not be sequential. Some suggest that Daniel may have crossed paths with Ezra. Ezra may have been active during the time of Esther and worked directly with Nehemiah. Daniel was in Susa (Daniel 8:2), Nehemiah was in Susa (Nehemiah 1:1), and the events of Esther happened in Susa (Esther 2:5).

About 586 B.C., Jerusalem fell and was destroyed by the Babylonians. Nebuchadnezzar died around 562 B.C. and Cyrus the Great captured Babylon around 540 B.C. and ruled until 530 B.C.[10] Several books of the Bible mention Cyrus and several prophets were active and included fasting in their words during this time.[11] Daniel served in several governments until the time of Cyrus (Daniel 1:21). Daniel 6:28 and 10:1 include events during the time of Cyrus. Israel began its return to Judea to rebuild the temple under Cyrus's rule around 540 B.C. (Ezra 1:1).

Darius (Cyrus's son-in-law?) and Artaxerxes (Artaxerxes I ruled 466-425 B.C.) are other rulers mentioned in Ezra 4:6, 6:14, Zechariah 7:1 and Daniel 9:1. Esther mentioned Ahasuerus as the king in Esther 1:1 and Ezra 4:6

---

10   Tavernier, Jan (2013). Some thoughts on Neo-Elamite Chronology. Arta, 2004.003, p. 27.

11   Search online for King Cyrus tomb in Iran and the Cyrus Cylinder at the British Museum. It is interesting.

(Ahasuerus in ESV) which may be Xerxes who ruled around 486-465 B.C.[12] Leaders during this period sometimes took the name of their father or predecessor, so tracking names and times is not conclusive.

Passages on fasting from the period of the captivity and beginning the return to Judah would include Jeremiah, Daniel, Zechariah, Ezra, Esther, and Nehemiah.

Ezra Prays and Fasts for Protection

The book of Ezra begins with King Cyrus granting the Jews permission to return and rebuild the temple. By chapter 4, the King mentioned was Artaxerxes. Due to some complaints, he stopped the temple work. The prophets Haggai and Zechariah get involved. By chapter 5, King Darius supports the finishing of the temple. King Artaxerxes gave Ezra, the priest, permission to return to Judah with treasures for the Temple, Ezra was ashamed to ask for soldiers for security on the trip. He had told the king of God's power and protection (Ezra 8:21-23). Therefore, the people who agreed to go fasted and asked God for protection on their trip. Ezra and his group were scared. It was a long journey, and they had precious cargo. They wanted to make sure God was aware of their danger. Appropriate fasting seems to add an emphasis to their prayers to God.

Esther Pleas for the Jews

If Ahasuerus in Ezra 4:6 is the same one mentioned in Esther, then the events from Esther would be before Ezra left for Judah. Esther is the Queen, but Haman has convinced King Ahasuerus to eliminate the Jews. When the Jews heard about the decree, they mourned, fasted, wept, lamented, and some wore sackcloth and ashes. When Esther decided to go to the king to plea for her people, she asked that all the Jews in Susa not eat or drink for three days and nights while she and her maids fasted. While Esther does not mention prayer for Jehovah's help, the context would indicate she sought God's protection and help (Esther 4:1-17).

Did Esther ask for a miracle, help in saying the right words, or a kind heart from King Ahasuerus? After Esther and supporters fast for three days, she asks the king to come to dinner. He comes that night, and she requests his company the next evening. After the king leaves Esther's dinner the first night, he cannot sleep, and the "bedtime story" he hears tells how Mordecai and Esther had saved him from an assassination attempt. The next day, Mordecai the Jew is honored by the king. Esther reveals the plot to kill

---

12 Historians have different opinions.

the Jews that evening after the king has just honored a Jew who had saved him! Esther pleas for the lives of the Jews. God provided the king with key information that opened his heart.

Esther and the Jews fasted, but why would servants fast with Esther? Esther's servants acted as her friends. When Esther joined the harem, she became friends with Hegai, who oversaw the ladies (Esther 2:8-9, 15). He helped her maximize her time and prepare for the king. Esther also gave credit to others. When Mordecai tells her about the plot to kill the king, she makes sure Mordecai receives the credit for the information that saved the king (Esther 2:22). Others appreciate this trait. Esther was isolated, and her servants were her only form of communication (Esther 4:4). This was a stressful time, and Esther probably included her servants for their support.

Ezra and Nehemiah Pray and Fast for Forgiveness

Once in Jerusalem, Ezra was shocked when he heard the Jews in the area had intermarried with Canaanites, Hittites, etc. Jehovah had sent Judah into captivity because they had not obeyed Him. God gave them another chance to return and serve him, and some disobeyed by marrying those who worship idols. Ezra showed concern by tearing his clothes, pulling his hair, and fasting (Ezra 9:1-15). Ezra's actions draw a crowd. Ezra wanted the people to realize how egregious their actions were. Sometimes, we become comfortable and immune to actions of friends or what we see in the media. Our biases close our hearts. An outsider sees it in a new light and provides a fresh perspective. Ezra saw what was happening and wanted to make sure others could see the problem. The people wept when they realized what they had allowed to happen. (I am really glad that pulling hair is not an action we do when we're upset!)

The leaders took an oath to put away foreign wives, and Ezra fasted and mourned all night (Ezra 10:1-6). After the public display, Ezra fasted and mourned privately. Ezra was leading the people through a critical time. Rabbinical scholars credit Ezra with bringing the Torah and Hebrew traditions from Babylon back to Jerusalem.[13] Ezra continues to mourn and fast to prepare to bring the Hebrews in Jerusalem back to serve Jehovah.

Nehemiah was a Jew in the city of Susa who served King Artaxerxes. Some men who had recently come from Judah told Nehemiah that the walls of Jerusalem were down, and the people were in trouble. Nehemiah wept, prayed, and fasted for days when he heard the bad news (Nehemiah 1:3-

---

13 Zucker, D. J. (2013). The Bible's Writings: An Introduction for Christians and Jews. Wipf and Stock Publishers. Eugene, Oregon, 139.

4). While serving King Artaxerxes, the king noticed Nehemiah was upset. The king's comment scared Nehemiah (Nehemiah 2:2). While serving the king, servants should not show any affliction. Nehemiah prayed to God and asked the king for help (Nehemiah 2:4-8). Nehemiah went to Jerusalem and organized the rebuilding of the city walls. Working with Ezra, the people confessed their sins, fasted, wore sackcloth, and put earth on their heads as a symbol of their penitence (Nehemiah 9:1).

Anna Looks for the Redemption of Jerusalem

About 450 years after Ezra, Luke talks about a prophet named Anna (Luke 2:36-38). She had been widowed at a young age and spent her life worshipping with fasting and prayer night and day. Luke says Anna did not depart from the temple. The Greek word interpreted "depart" in this passage also means desert or fall away. I tend to think Luke meant that Anna did not desert or quit worshipping at the Temple. Also, Anna would be limited to areas that allowed women, so she would not have been in some of the holy areas.

It is not likely that this was a total fast of no food or drink for many years. Anna may have done a "partial" fast where she ate a limited diet such as Daniel's twenty-one day fast (Daniel 10:1-3) but for years! The Greek word used for fasting may be interpreted as abstinence. Anna abstained from food and drink that others routinely partook. She was looking for the redemption of Israel. What kind of heart would spend decades focused on the condition of her people? Eventually, Anna saw the Messiah and gave thanks to God! Can you see her excitement? After years of prayer, she could tell others that the redemption of Jerusalem had come! (Luke 2:36-38).[14]

Preparing for Challenges

Matthew 4:2 talks about how Jesus prepared for his ministry. He separated from everyone, went to the wilderness, fasted, and prayed. This was before he began teaching the world.

Later, at the end of Jesus' ministry Jesus eats the Passover with his disciples. At the end, he tells them that he will not drink any fruit of the vine until he is with them in the kingdom (Matthew 26:29; Mark 14:25; Luke 22:18). They sing, go to Gethsemane, and Jesus prays. While on the cross, Jesus is offered a sponge with sour wine. They put it on his lips (he didn't drink), and he gave up his spirit (John 19:30). After Jesus is risen, he cooks breakfast

---

[14] Anna was from the tribe of Asher. Since Asher was one of the tribes in Israel taken into captivity by the Assyrians, her family may have moved to Judah before Israel was assimilated.

for some disciples by the Sea of Tiberias (John 21:1-15). The kingdom has come.

It seems fasting was part of Jesus' preparation for a particularly challenging period. In sports, participants focus and go through routines that put them at their best for the event. For Jesus, fasting and communing with God was how he prepared. Fasting is a tool to help up know that God sees our deep concern. It is a physical action to express our spiritual desire. Going into a spiritual challenge requires as much help as would a physical battle. We can use Jesus' tools to do the same for us spiritually!

Saul (Paul) Prays and Fasts

Saul was headed to Damascus when Jesus stopped him 'in his tracks' (Acts 9). For three days, Saul could not see, and he did not eat or drink (Acts 9:3-9). Saul's beliefs had been turned upside down, quite a paradigm shift. Just as Esther and her friends did before she went to save her people, Saul didn't eat or drink for three days. Jesus gave Saul his mission: open the eyes of the Gentiles to receive the remission of sins (Acts 26:15-18). Jesus talked to Ananias and sent him to help Saul see clearly. Saul was baptized, and then he ate (Acts 9:10-19).

Summary

We have looked at about 46 examples of fasting in the Old and New Testaments. Paul and David fasted the most, although Anna's lifetime of fasting is impressive. Daniel received direct responses from messengers from God which was not common. Moses, Elijah, and Jesus shared many challenges including fasts of forty days. Leaders called fasts when threatened and to rededicate themselves to Jehovah (Samuel and Ezra). Some fasts were due to distress caused by their circumstances. Paul and Barnabas prayed and fasted with the churches when selecting leaders. Next, we look at the passages that discuss appropriate and unacceptable fasts.

Fasting Expectations

This section includes scriptures on fasting with feedback from Jehovah to the people and teachings by Jesus.

Jews Fast on Day of Atonement

One of the required holy days in Judaism is the day of Atonement (Yom Kippur) which is primarily based on Leviticus 23:26-32. The day (evening to evening or 25 hours) is a day of no work, affliction, sacrifice, and atonement for sins. Some consider this to be the only required fast in Judaism. It is an annual memorial, but not mentioned frequently in the Old Testament (Leviticus 16:30-31; 23:27-32; Numbers 29:7-11). The word fast is not used in these passages, but the word "afflict." According to Strong's Hebrew dictionary, afflict includes the synonyms to abase, chasten, humble, or submit self. It refers to the Jew's 400 years of slavery in Egypt (Genesis 15:13; Deuteronomy 26:6), and Hagai's desired response to Sara (Genesis 16:9). The psalmist in Psalms 119:67 says that "before I was afflicted, I went astray: but now I have kept thy word." In verse 71, the writer suggests, "It is good for me that I have been afflicted; that I might learn thy statutes." These thoughts imply the power of affliction in helping us focus on God.

Isaiah chastises Israel for fasting but not really afflicting their selves (Isaiah 58:3-5). After Daniel's partial fast in Daniel 10, he afflicted himself; therefore, God sent a messenger to him (Daniel 10:12). James 4:9 says, "be afflicted and mourn and weep: let your laughter be turned to mourning, and your joy to sorrow" (ASV). The Greek word to be afflicted is a similar concept to the term afflicted in the Old Testament. While not a call to specifically fast, James uses wording that the Jews would recognize from the Old Testament.

The Day of Atonement is not just a fast from eating or drinking but about humbling "self." A day of affliction for the sins of the year. There are different actions by some groups. There is usually no eating or drinking, not even water, no marital relations, bathing, applying lotions, and some do not wear leather shoes and suggest participants wear white as a sign of purity.[15] Some suggest abstinence from electronics also during this time. The concept asks that participants humble themselves, control their desires, and spend a day realizing that Jehovah will judge and we need his forgiveness.

---

15 Reich, A. (2022). "Yom Kippur: What is the Day of Atonement, the Holiest Jewish Holiday." https://www.jpost.com/judaism/article-718747.

Calls to Repent, Fast

The prophet Joel calls for God's people to repent, consecrate a fast, and cry out to the Lord (Joel 1;13-14). He shows them that the locusts are a warning from the Lord for them to change and return to the Lord before it gets worse. Fasting is part of their cry for the Lord's mercy. Later, Joel asks them again to return to the Lord with all their heart, fasting, weeping, and mourning (2:12-16). After they have changed their heart, they fast as a demonstration of their intent. By verse 15, Joel includes everyone in the call to return to the Lord, participate in a group fast, and assemble so the people do not become a "byword" by other nations.[16]

Joel asks that the people put Jehovah first. Weeping, mourning, and fasting were how they illustrate their change of heart. Joel asks for a spiritual change and a physical expression of it. It is somewhat like baptism—a physical expression of our repentance and choice to follow Christ.

Unacceptable Fasts

Isaiah talks about why Israel's fast and Sabbaths were unacceptable (Isaiah 58). Israel feels they are doing what Jehovah had asked. Verse 3 begins with their complaint: "'Why have we fasted,' they say, 'and You have not seen? Why have we afflicted our souls, and You take no notice?' 'In fact, in the day of your fast you find pleasure, And exploit all your laborers. Indeed you fast for strife and debate, And to strike with the fist of wickedness. You will not fast as you do this day, To make your voice heard on high'" (Isaiah 58:3-4). The people expected their fasting to give them a response from Jehovah; God would hear their prayers. However, their fasts were not about seeking God's will but their own pleasure. They wanted God to answer their supplications, but they continued to oppress the weak, fought with each other, and ignored His will.

God gives instructions on what he expects in Isaiah 58:5-7, "'Is it a fast that I have chosen, A day for a man to afflict his soul? Is it to bow down his head like a bulrush, And to spread out sackcloth and ashes? Would you call this a fast, And an acceptable day to the LORD? 'Is this not the fast that I have chosen: To loose the bonds of wickedness, To undo the heavy burdens, To let the oppressed go free, And that you break every yoke? Is it not to share your bread with the hungry, And that you bring to your house the poor who are cast out; When you see the naked, that you cover him, And not hide

---

16 Moses's law only required the Jews to assemble as a group a few days each year. Therefore, calling for an assembly of everyone underlines the emergency they were facing. The weekly Sabbath was a home event.

yourself from your own flesh?'" An acceptable fast begins with humbling ourselves to God and then acting in a manner that glorifies God. Fasting is not just about us but our actions to others as well.

During Jeremiah's time, Judah continued to have issues with fasting. God tells the people through Jeremiah that they have wandered and have not restrained their feet. He will no longer hear their cry or accept their offerings. While fasting in the past may have helped God hear their cries, it no longer made a difference. It is scary to see what happens when God removes his protection. When we ignore the Lord, afflicting ourselves (fasting) will not make him listen (Jerimiah 14:10-12).

By the time Nebuchadnezzar ruled Babylon, things were so bad in Judah that Jeremiah was not allowed in the house of the Lord. So, during the day of fasting, when the people gathered, Baruch (Jeremiah's scribe) read the words Jehovah had given to Jeremiah to share. It was not received well by the leaders, and King Jehoiakim (the son of King Josiah) cut the scroll and threw it into the fire. He tried to seize Jeremiah and Baruch, but Jehovah hid them (Jerimiah 36:5-26).

The people were fasting. Isn't that what Joel and Isaiah had asked them to do? In Jeremiah 37:2, a new king is mentioned, but he and the people do not listen to the words of the Lord. The people may have performed some of the acts of worship, but their heart was not following Jehovah. A concern is that fasting becomes a physical act without a heart and deeds that seek to exalt God.

When Jesus teaches about fasting in the "Sermon on the Mount," he warns the audience that fasting to be seen by others will not be effective (Matthew 6:16). In Luke, Jesus recounts a parable about a Pharisee who prays his thankfulness that he is not like other men who do obvious sins. He concludes with pride his actions, fasting twice a week and giving tithes (Luke 18:9-14).

The Pharisee may have improved his metabolism and lowered food costs, but his fasting did not begin with humility. He wasn't thankful for how he had helped the needy or the oppressed. He was thankful that he wasn't like some sinners and that he tithed (required) and fasted weekly (not required). Moses' law did not include weekly fasting. The Pharisees seem to apply the "if some is good, more is better" rule. Fasting doesn't make us more acceptable to God or better than others. Jesus points out that not all fasts are helpful in our relationship with Him.

God's Expectations

While in Babylonian captivity, the Jews added fasts to mourn the destruction of the temple and the death of Gedaliah.[17] In Zechariah 7:3, the people ask if they need to keep the memorials and fasts now that people are going back to Jerusalem. In Zechariah 5 and 6, the prophet answers their question with a question. Did you fast for God or yourselves? God wanted them to explain why they were fasting. Were they sorry they had failed God or lost their homes? It seems that fasting for the wrong reasons does not add value to our relationship with God.

Later in chapter 7:9-10, the Lord tells them what is more important than mourning and fasting.

1. Execute true judgment.
2. Be merciful and kind to others.
3. Do not oppress widows, fatherless, strangers, or poor.
4. Do not devise evil against others.

The people refused to pay attention, turned aside, and stopped their ears (Zechariah 7:11). Ignoring these precepts and hardening their hearts, not hearing or doing the law, and ignoring the prophets prompted God to scatter them (Zechariah 7:12-14).

When Jesus Is Not with You

Fasting during Jesus's time was not unusual as John the Baptizer's disciples fasted and Pharisees fasted (Mark 2:18-20; Matthew 9:14-15; and Luke 5:33-35). Matthew, Mark, and Luke all record a question to Jesus about why his disciples didn't fast. Jesus responds that it is not appropriate to fast while he (the Bridegroom) is with them. However, Jesus says his disciples will fast when he is no longer with them.

Why would it be inappropriate to fast when Jesus is with you? Fasting is an action added to worship, a prayer, supplication, or a request to God. It is a physical action that shows our food is from God, not just bread. Jesus's disciples had a unique relationship with God during this time and did not need fasting to improve their relationship with God. God was with them.

---

17 Gedaliah was appointed Governor of Judah by Nebuchadnezzar and was murdered (2 Kings 25:22; Jeremiah 41:2-3).

Fast to the Father

In the sermon on the mount, Jesus's teachings and actions drew all people to him. People from Galilee, Decapolis, Jerusalem, Judea, and beyond the Jordan were coming to hear Him (Matthew 4:25). In his sermon, Jesus teaches that "when you give...," do it for God's appreciation, not man's (Matthew 6:2-4). Additionally, "when you pray...," do it privately and keep it succinct (Matthew 6:6-8).[18] Finally, "when you fast...," don't make a show about it, but fast to the Lord for his approval (Matthew 6:17-18). Jesus closes his sermon with an admonition to hear his words and do them so you will be like a wise man (Matthew 7:24).

Matthew 6:3,5, and 16 all begin with the phrase: "When you give..., When you pray..., When you fast..." It indicates an expectation that the listeners will do these actions. Jesus follows with instructions on how to avoid common mistakes and make them more effective. Don't fast for the praise of others (Matthew 6:16). Look normal and fast to be seen by the Father (Matthew 6:17-18). People who fast to receive the appreciation of others are not improving their relationship with God. They are about self-praise.

An example is the parable of the Pharisee and the tax collector (Luke 18:11-12). Jesus told the people that the fasting they see by others does not improve their spiritual bond with God. Jesus closes this discussion on fasting with the promise that God will respond to the fast and prayer when done well. That is a wonderful promise.

What Is Not Taught to Christians about Fasting

There is no routine, required fasts for Christians in the scriptures (e.g., Day of Atonement, Lent, or Good Friday). When Christians raised under the Law of Moses tried to add circumcision and keeping the Law of Moses to the expectation of Christians, a council gathered at Jerusalem (Acts 15:1-6). The leaders sent a letter to the new churches that Paul and Barnabas had recently established. Christians did not need to be circumcised or follow the Law of Moses. Christians are not expected to follow Jewish holy days fasts/feasts. They need to abstain from eating idol sacrifices, blood, things strangled, and fornication (Acts 15:28-29). While not added by the council, it could be implied that all Christians (disciples of Christ) would follow the teachings of Jesus. The church at Antioch fasted, and individual groups fasted, but not on any schedule or specifications. Jesus fasted. Paul and Barnabas fasted, but there are no commands to fast weekly, annually, or upon any events.

---

18   This is followed with an example of a prayer in Matthew 6:9-13.

Fasts are not specified as to length. While evening to evening might be a traditional day fast for the Jews, there are examples of shorter or longer periods in the Old Testament examples. The examples by Christians do not provide a specific example of time to fast.

Fasts are not specified as to what is to be abstained. Some fasts specify no food or drink, but others, such as Daniel's fasts, are more about abstaining from certain foods and actions. Anna likely abstained from certain foods/activities over her years of fasting.

Fasting is not part of a checklist that makes you an "active" or "in-service" Christian. Fasting more or routinely does not make one more spiritual (see Pharisee in Luke 18:9-14). Fasting is unacceptable or ignored by God if done inappropriately (Isaiah 58:3-6; Jeremiah 14:10-12).

Miscellaneous Points on Fasting

Health Benefits of Fasting

Spiritual fasts are not for health reasons. In the last few years, intermittent fasting has become popular as an option to lose weight and improve health. The Bible does not include health as a reason to fast. A Christian practice of moderation and self-control would lead to better health for most, but it is not the objective of a fast to Jehovah.

Several Biblical teachings have benefits beyond our relationship with God. Let's focus on Jesus's teachings from Matthew 6: giving, prayer, forgiveness, and fasting. According to the Cleveland Clinic, giving increases serotonin, dopamine, and oxytocin. These chemicals in your brain help to regulate your mood, give you a sense of pleasure, and increase your connection with others. Some found it lowered blood pressure and decreased stress.[19] You have probably felt an improvement in your mood when you give or help others. A 2011 study by Bremner, Koole, and Bushman found prayer reduced anger and aggression for those who prayed for others.[20] This is not surprising to those who pray, but does provide support for the benefits of prayer, which brings up the benefits of forgiveness. Dr. Karen Swartz from Johns Hopkins Mood Disorders Center notes that studies see lower risk of

---

[19] Albers, Susan, PsyD., (2022). "Why Giving is good for your Health." Cleveland Clinic, healthessentials, https://health.clevelandclinic.org/why-giving-is-good-for-your-health/.

[20] Bremner, R. H., Koole, S. L., & Bushman, B. J. (2011). "Pray for those who mistreat you: Effects of prayer on anger and aggression." Personality and Social Psychology Bulletin, 37(6), 830-837.

heart attack, improved cholesterol levels, better sleep, reduced pain, anxiety, depression, and stress linked to forgiveness.[21] Do you sleep better if you have forgiven a wrong? Forgiveness is a secret weapon for Christians.

Finally, Jesus mentions fasting should be done in secret (Matthew 6:16-18). Fasting may have some physical benefits for some people, but results vary. There are different kinds of fasts. The Christian Orthodox Church fast focuses on fruits, vegetables, legumes, and fish and may be followed for 18 to 200 days. Health benefits are similar to those following a Mediterranean diet.[22] One finding was that after the fast, participants continued to have a healthier dietary intake, providing long-term benefits. A study from The New England Journal of Medicine from 2019 found long-term benefits to animals that use intermittent fasting. Human studies over short-term practice for overweight young and middle-aged adults reveal benefits due to metabolic switching and cellular stress resistance that help lose weight.[23] Antidotal comments indicate practicing fasting improves self-discipline.

There are many benefits to being a Christian. A Christian life is awesome. We have family and friends who share values. We have a mighty God who listens to YOU. Not only powerful but a God who is good and merciful. It is not surprising that doing what he teaches is good for us currently and in the future.

Fasting in Different Areas and Purposes

As discussed previously, fasts are used by some to improve health and by different cultures and religions. According to the Encyclopedia Britannica, fasting is prevalent historically and frequently practiced today. Fasting was part of penance and confession in the pre-Columbian religion of Peru. Native American tribes would fast before their "vision quest." Buddhists fast with meditation, while the Hindus include frequent fasts by their spiritual leaders. The Greeks fasted to seek revelation from some of their gods. Islam includes annual fasting during the month of Ramadan. Catholic traditions include abstinence during Lent and some fasting on Good Friday.

---

21 Karen Swartz. "Forgiveness: Your Health Depends on It," Johns Hopkins Medicine, https://www.hopkinsmedicine.org/health/wellness-and-prevention/forgiveness-your-health-depends-on-it.
22 Kokkinopoulou, A., Pagkalos, I., Hassapidou, M., & Kafatos, A. (2022). Dietary patterns in adults following the Christian orthodox fasting regime in Greece. Frontiers in Nutrition, 9.
23 De Cabo, R., & Mattson, M. P. (2019). Effects of intermittent fasting on health, aging, and disease. New England Journal of Medicine, 381(26), 2541-2551.

Fasts have been used to bring awareness to issues historically. In 1981, Irish nationalists used hunger strikes to urge awareness of political prisoners. Mahatma Gandhi used fasts to publicize his objectives. In the 1960s, fasts were used to protest civil rights issues.

Different Source Material

Because of different source material, the King James translation has some additional mentions of fasting in the New Testament.[24] If you use the King James translation, in Matthew 17:14-21 and Mark 9:14-29 a boy possessed by a demon could not be cured by the disciples. Jesus explains that their failure was linked to belief or their lack of it. The King James text adds a requirement of prayer and fasting in an additional verse that other translations may not include.

Also, in the King James version, Cornelius is fasting and praying when a messenger tells him to send for Peter (Acts 10:30). Most modern translations mention prayer, but not fasting.

Finally, in 1 Corinthians 7:5, a married couple who is struggling might agree to separate temporarily and focus on prayer and fasting. Again, other translations do not include fasting in addition to prayer.

Forced Abstinence

Paul writes to the Corinthians about his efforts including a list of physical hardships and spiritual strengths. Fasting is included in 2 Corinthians 6:5 and 11:27. These allude to forced fasting during his struggles. However, he may be mentioning his choice to fast. You decide.

Hermeneutics

There are some hermeneutic approaches to fasting that may be discussed in a topical Bible study. Are there any commands? Are there apostolic examples? Is there a necessary inference on the practice? How does the practice differ in the Patriarchal, Mosaical, and Christian dispensations? Finally, what is the historical context, and are there grammatical nuances that impact understanding?

---

24 The King James Version is translated from the Antioch text, while other translations use the Alexandrian text.

There are examples of Jesus, the apostle Paul, Barnabas, Christians in Antioch and Iconium, Lystra, and Antioch of Pisida fasting with other actions. There is no specific day to fast as in the Mosaic teachings. In the Old Testament, the writers use a word that means to 'cover over' mouth or a word for fasting. When discussing the Day of Atonement, the people are to afflict themselves. In practice, this embraces a fast, but the word or command to fast is not included. James writes to draw near to God, purify your hearts, be afflicted, mourn, weep, humble yourselves, and God will exalt you (4:8-10). The term afflicted and the context is similar to the attitude when Jews were called to atone for their sins. Is there a command to fast? Maybe a better question is, how can we follow James' advice? I encourage you to study the passages and context.

A discussion on fasting is not to be avoided! Jesus practiced and taught about fasting. Christians practiced fasting. The Old Testament provides examples of effectual fasts, ineffective fasts, and what God expects. Other than the Day of Atonement for the Jews, fasts varied in time, and what was abstained differed. It is a tool used by many effectively and is a topic worth your study time.

How Can Fasting Help?

It takes time to answer the personal question. If you have never fasted, you may find a time when fasting supports a prayer you feel about intensely. Most fasts have an emotional need (Moses, Hannah, Jonathan, David, Ahab, Ninevites, King Darius, Ezra, Nehemiah, and Paul). In difficult times, we may be so upset that we don't want food or drink. All we want is to pray and talk to our Father. We automatically eliminate the physical to focus on God.

When it comes to having a relationship with Jehovah, David and Daniel stand out. There are many scriptures about David's actions and from the Psalms David's feelings. David fasted when friends died, enemies died, people were sick, his son was dying, he was scared, and when he felt oppressed. David's prayers frequently included fasts. Daniel prayed routinely, but when he fasted and prayed, God sent angels to explain. That is a relationship with God! These examples illustrate how fasting and prayer can make an impact.

Paul talks about self-control in many passages (Romans 6:12; 1 Thessalonians 4:4; Philippians 2:14-16). In 1 Corinthians 9:27, he talks about how he disciplines his body to "keep it under control." In Galatians 5:22-23, the fruit of the Spirit includes self-control. Paul is also included in all the examples of Christians fasting in the New Testament. If you have tried fasting for a day and failed, you understand the self-control it takes. Try fasting part of the day or partial fasting. Fasting with others is a practice shown by New Testament Christians. Doing actions with others helps many to be more successful. If you had been taught as a child how to fast for 25 hours routinely, would that help your self-discipline? Is restraint a needed skill to live as a Christian in the world?

Fasting is a tool to supplement prayer, mourning, supplications, and worship of God. You may want to give God a 'heads-up' about an issue you feel strongly about. Adding fasting to prayer increases the time spent thinking and praying about the concern during the day. Old Testament examples fasted when there was intense distress. It seems to add an exclamation point to whatever they wanted to share with God. It is a tool that can continue to be effective in all eras.

Summary and Concluding Thoughts

Our focus on fasting scriptures began with Moses fasting for 40 days while receiving the 10 Commandments. The Law of Moses included an annual day for Jews to afflict and humble themselves. Each year on the Day of Atonement, participating Jews fasted and abstained to focus on God's mercy and power. Over time, as Israel struggled with sin, they would ask for God's help or rededicate to Jehovah with fasting and prayers. God responded and supported Israel against their foes. When Jonah told the Assyrians they would be judged, the Ninevites repented and fasted. When Elijah told Ahab God's judgment on his sins, Ahab humbled himself and fasted. In both cases, God relented and gave them time.

There are multiple reasons to fast. Individuals may fast when they are upset and realize they need God. When David wanted to change God's mind, he fasted and prayed for a week. David mentioned fasting several times in his Psalms. He fasted when he was in need and for friends who were sick. David and others fasted to mourn and honor slain leaders. Daniel had several times where he "afflicted" himself to understand God's plan for his people. Anna spent most of her life seeking the redemption of Israel with fasting and worshipping.[25]

Several prophets call on the people to fast and return to Jehovah, but appropriately. Prophets chastised Jews for fasts that did not include true judgment, mercy, or kindness. They would fast to the Lord but oppress the weak and poor while devising evil plans. King Saul didn't fast to the Lord but to manipulate his men for his agenda.

[25] When quantifying the number of days mentioned to fast, the "Hall of Fame" winners for fasting from the scriptures would include Moses, David, Daniel, Anna and Paul. Quite a select group.

While in Babylon, the Jews added fasts and other traditional actions. By the time of Jesus, fasting was a common religious practice. John's disciples fasted, as did the Pharisees. Some Pharisees fasted publicly to show others how pious they were. Jesus taught his disciples to fast privately, and the Lord will reward them.

Jesus and Moses lived on the word of God (fasted for forty days) before they shared their teachings with the Jews. Paul, Barnabas, and leaders at Antioch fasted and prayed before Paul and Barnabas left to teach the Gentiles. Esther, servants, and the Jews at Susa fasted before she approached the King. Ezra and Nehemiah fasted when they realized the sins of the people in Jerusalem. These are examples of how fasting and spending time with God is a good practice before challenging times.

There are no commands to fast routinely or time limits on fasting for Christians. There are Bible examples of fasts for forty days, three days, one day, or part of a day. Fasting is a physical action complimenting a spiritual action. It is not an activity to be done for itself. The Bible mentions fasting along with worship, prayer, supplication, mourning, confession, remembrance, protection, forgiveness, praise, guidance, or re-dedication to God. From the Old Testament, we see reasons for fasts varied, times varied, and what was abstained from fasting varied. God will not listen to those who fast but fail to humble themselves or continue to sin (Isaiah 58:3-6). David and Daniel were powerful prayers and frequently added fasts to their supplications to Jehovah. In the New Testament, Jesus teaches that his disciples will fast when he is no longer with them. Paul, Barnabas, and early Christians fasted, worshipped, and prayed. (Acts 13:1-2; 14:23). Fasts are very flexible actions. What seems to be required is a need to bring something to God's attention and a willingness to humble yourself and align to HIS will.

Appendix

Commonalities of Moses, Elijah, and Jesus

In addition to fasting for forty days, Moses, Elijah, and Jesus talked among themselves (Mark 9:2-13). This is amazing to consider leaders from such different times sharing their thoughts. Were they comparing who was dealing with the most stubborn Jews? Was Moses and Elijah giving Jesus support? The scripture does not give details, but it will be something to ask. In addition to fasting for forty days and their conversation recorded in Mark, Jesus, Moses, and Elijah had several commonalities:
    1. Fasted forty days. They literally lived from the word of God.
    2. Spoke together after Moses and Elijah had died (Mark 9:2-13). They

met and were seen by Peter, James, and John. How do you think Peter and the others recognized Elijah and Moses?
3. Their physical bodies were all protected.
   When Moses died, God buried him on Mount Nebo (Deuteronomy 34:5-6). Jude adds a note about how the archangel Michael rebuked the devil over the body of Moses (Jude 1:9). This seems to indicate, for some reason, the body of Moses was of interest to the devil and was protected. Elijah's body was taken by chariots of fire (2 Kings 2:1-14). Of course, Jesus was raised from the dead.
4. Talked with God directly.
   Numbers 12 talks about how Miriam and Aaron were disparaging Moses. God intervenes and explains how he talks to Moses directly, not through visions or dreams as he does with other prophets (Numbers 12:6-9). We've already talked about God's conversation with Elijah in 1 Kings 19:9-18. Since Jesus is God, this seems redundant, but the voice from heaven when Jesus was baptized was a direct communication to Jesus and those with him (Matthew 3:13-17).
5. Others sought to kill them.
   Moses left Egypt since Pharaoh was trying to kill him (Exodus 2:15). Jezebel had vowed to kill Elijah (1 Kings 19:2). And multiple times, people tried to seize or kill Jesus: John 5:18; 7:1,19-25; 8:59; 10:31; 11:53; Luke 13:31; Mark 14:1.
6. Leaders of their dispensations/era.
   Moses brought the Mosaic law. Elijah is considered a leader of the prophets. In 2 Kings 2:15, when the sons of the prophets saw that Elisha had taken Elijah's responsibility, they bowed to him. This seems to indicate Elijah's prior leadership of the prophets. Jesus established the Christian relationship to God.
7. Separated from others to spend time with God.
   Moses went on the mountain alone, Elijah was alone in the wilderness (1 Kings 17:1-7), and Jesus went to the mountain to pray (Matthew 14:23, Mark 6:46; Luke 6:12; John 6:15).
8. Faced several common challenges.
   They struggled with those they were leading. The Hebrews, coming from Egypt and during the time of Ahab, did not have a strong relationship with Jehovah. In Mark 9:14-19 after Jesus has shared some time with Moses and Elijah (Mark 9:2-8), he comes down to see the disciples arguing. Jesus seems to vent his frustration in Mark 9:19: "O faithless generation, how long am I to be with you? How long am I to bear with you? Bring him to me." Spiritual leaders today may have empathy for these leaders.

Appendix

Group Fasts

There are examples of group fasts by Israel or Judah (multiple occasions), Saul's army, David's men, people of Jabesh-Gilead, Ninevites, and Esther's maids. In the New Testament, John's disciples, disciples of the Pharisees, Christians at Antioch, Paul, Barnabas, and elders at Lystra, Iconium, and Antioch Pisidia are mentioned as fasting with prayers or worship. The table lists the people who fasted, their objectives, accompanying actions, and outcomes. Some events do not clearly explain the reasons for the fasts. Most ask God for help or forgiveness. Fasting seems to add a physical aspect to a spiritual request. See chart on the following two pages.

		Objective	Actions with Fasting	Outcomes
Leviticus 23:26-32	Jews on Day of Atonement	A day to afflict and humble yourself to the Lord	No work, rest	Renew relationship and recognize debt to Jehovah
Judges 20:26-28	Israel	Israel fighting Benjamin asks what to do after two days of losses.	Wept, offered burnt and peace offerings to Jehovah	Told to fight a third day. They followed the Lord's directions and won the conflict.
1 Samuel 7:3	Israel	Israel rededicating to Jehovah.	Idols put away, prayer, cleansing	The Lord defeated the Philistines.
2 Chronicles 20:3	Israel	Jehoshaphat was afraid of the Moabites & Ammonites	All Judah assembled to pray for God's help	Spirit came to Jahaziel who gave directions on how God would defeat their enemies.
1 Samuel 14:24-30	Saul's Army	Saul wanted to avenge enemies	Unknown	After defeating the enemies, the men killed sheep and ate raw (with blood) because they were so hungry.
1 Samuel 31:13 and 1 Chronicles 10:12	People from Jabesh-gilead	Honor Saul and his sons who had saved them from the Ammonites	Buried Saul and his sons who had died in battle	David blessed them for their actions. (2 Sam 2:5).
Jonah 3:5, 4:	Ninevites	Ask Jehovah for mercy	A call for everyone to turn from evil and violence. People wore sackcloth	Ninevites were given mercy.

Appendix

		Objective	Actions with Fasting	Outcomes
Esther 4:1-17	Esther, her maids, and Jews in Susa	Ask Jehovah to deliver the Jews from Haman's plan for their destruction	Fast together. Probably prayed to the Lord	Esther successfully revealed Haman's plan and the King recognized Mordecai's loyalty.
Ezra 8:21-23	Ezra and those traveling to Jerusalem	Safe passage to Jerusalem to honor His name	Humbled themselves, asked God for his protection	God listened and gave Ezra's group a safe journey to Jerusalem
Nehemiah 9:1	People in Jerusalem	Asked Jehovah for forgiveness	Wore sackcloth, dirt on their heads, separated from foreigners, confessed their sins and the iniquities of their fathers. Listened to the word for several hours and worshiped the Lord.	The wall was completed (Neh. 12:27) and the people worshiped Jehovah in the Temple (Neh. 12:44-47)
Acts 13:2-3	Christians at Antioch	Unknown	Worship	message from Holy Spirit
Acts 14:21-23	Churches at Derbe, Iconium, Lystra, and Antioch of Pisida	Install Elders to lead the local church	Prayer	Letter to Galatia and visit by Paul and Silas later, where he mentions Timothy (Acts 16:1) Gaius of Derbe and Timothy accompanied Paul (Acts 20:4)

Individual Fasts

The Old Testament mentions Moses, Hannah, Jonathan, David, Elijah, Daniel, Nehemiah, Ezra, Ahab, King Darius, Nazirites fasted individually. Likewise in the New Testament, Anna, Jesus, a Pharisee, and Saul/Paul fasted. The individual fasts may be for others or for self. The table lists the individuals who fasted and why they choose to fast.

Why Individuals Fast?	
Moses	save Israel & Aaron
Elijah	travel to Mount Horeb
Jesus	prepare for ministry
Nazirite	separate themselves
Hannah	distressed
Jonathan	distressed
David	honor fallen
David	ask for life of son
David	friends are sick
Ahab	keep punishment from him
King Darius	save Daniel
Daniel	save Jerusalem
Daniel	questions about the future for the Jews?
Ezra	sins of people
Nehemiah	sins of people
Anna	see God's redemption
Saul (Paul)	scared

www.ingramcontent.com/pod-product-compliance
Lightning Source LLC
LaVergne TN
LVHW020940090426
835512LV00020B/3440